I0750275

FINISHING LINE PRESS
www.finishinglinepress.com

SELLING THE FAMILY

poems by

Nancy Kay Peterson

Finishing Line Press
Georgetown, Kentucky

SELLING THE FAMILY

ISBN 978-1-64662-402-7 First Edition

ACKNOWLEDGMENTS

"Resignation Affirmation" appeared online (as "Resignation") on *One Sentence Poems* in May 2019.

Publisher: Leah Huete de Maines

Editor: Christen Kincaid

Cover Art: Nancy Kay Peterson

Author Photo: Nancy Kay Peterson

Cover Design: Elizabeth Maines McCleavy

Order online: www.finishinglinepress.com
also available on amazon.com

Author inquiries and mail orders:
Finishing Line Press
PO Box 1626
Georgetown, Kentucky 40324
USA

Table of Contents

Dedicated to the Petersons

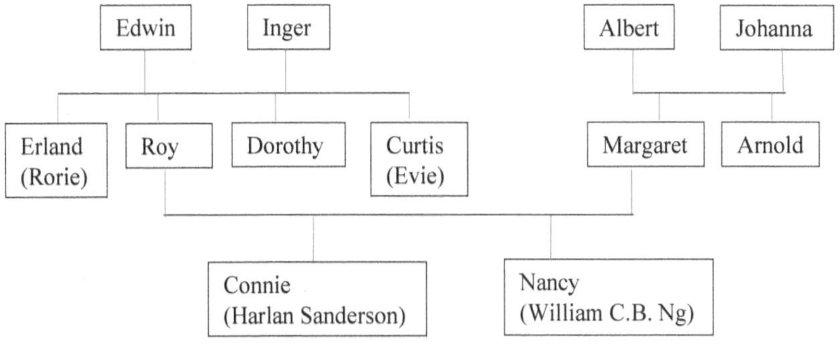

Keeping Watch

When visiting Mother,
I am often afraid
to look out the window
of my parents' house
before I intend to.
I still expect
to see my father
striding bow-legged
towards home, kicking stones
along the gravel drive.

If I were to see him,
it would be there, outside,
but this evening's scene
holds only meager winter.
I am relieved,
yet hesitant to linger
in case his shape
should coalesce
out of the darkness.

I am not afraid of him,
but of missing him too much.

Written at Grizzly Adams Restaurant Six Days Later

The only time
I remember looking
into Mother's eyes
she lay dying..

They were the deep brown
of stained walnut,
mainly unknowing,
though at times through the pain,
past the Alzheimer's,
flared sparks of recognition,
less fleeting than a gasp,
much less than the breath
she struggled for.

I watched her eyes widen,
confusion and fear doubling,
heard her cries for help,
one arm reaching for
her long-dead twin,
Arnold, Arnold, Arnold.

I said go to him,
apologized for not being able
to help her leave
and held her hand.

My Only Sister is Dying

I leave the nursing home,
drive along winding country roads.
The trees are bare,
the sky the color
of an old woman's hair,
the bluffs, bared breasts
mottled with barren oak age spots.
Pines line up like green biopsy scars.
Oh, to be free of growing old,
to boldly face the years,
the fear of that final alone
that comes to us all,
the one thing we share
that we cannot share,
our fading and falling,
our solo souls bared.

My Widower Brother-in-Law

The Meal on Wheels people called.
He had not answered the door.
Ninety miles away, I worked the phone,
to find someone to investigate.

The cop called, apologizing, said
he hated to do this
over the phone, tell me
what by then I already knew.

As we spoke long distance
about what to do, when to come,
a friend arrived at that end, volunteered
to adopt the frightened dog and cat.

The next day, my husband and I went
to find the happy-hour ice cream box
melted on the kitchen counter,
beside the happy-hour pet treats.

The friend John, who'd been there, later said
Harlan had looked like he was at peace.
He would not have to endure the upcoming
anniversary of my sister's death.

I pray
I can endure
both hers
and his.

Being Last

Imagine being last.
No one to call on Christmas.
No packages under a fragrant pine.

Little but
time to fill
day after day
after day.

Who will buy a coffin,
make final arrangements,
chance upon the writings,
save them for discovery?

My heart knows my work
will be simply discarded.
What stranger would read them,
a lifetime of poems?

Disposing of My Sister's 45-Year-Long Marriage

My father and brother-in-law
converted the dirt-floor chicken coop
into a red barn *sommer hytte,*
with electricity, plumbing
and wood burning stove,
and sleeping loft reached by climbing
ladder-like steps flanked by a railing made
from a stripped, twisted branch.

Sister and brother-in-law
spent summers here,
with Boots, the border collie,
Pepper, the poodle mutt,
two white cats, Sugar and Spice,
and sometime guest little sister. Me.

The barn became storage space
for things never thrown away,
left to mold in summer humidity,
sustaining mice and spiders,
attracting Asian beetles
by the thousands.

For two years on summer Saturdays,
in musty, dust-laden air,
I sorted, discarded and salvaged
photographs from parents and parents' parents
1950s collector toys, bar trinkets,
antique spittoons, kerosene lanterns,
old washing tubs, bottles, suitcases,

twenty-two decaying purses,
rolls of leftover wallpaper,
hundreds of mouse-stained books,
boxes of dishes, broken appliances,
warped wooden skis, a toboggin,

vacation mementos,
a shedding reindeer skin from
their honeymoon in Norway,
shoe-boxed, yellowing love letters
he had written her fifty years ago;

all things to be judged equally
as saleable or forever worthless.

Auctioneers' Treasure Search

A century of farm tools from his father,
a lathe from my grandfather, the diemaker,
antique wall phones from Dad's career
working for the phone company,

Dozens of hammers, wrenches, screwdrivers,
tape measures, screws, nails, frayed ropes,
rusted pitchforks, broken shovel handles,
knotted electric cords, old push lawnmowers,

mostly fodder for the yawning dumpster.

In the rafters, a one-horse cutter, and
mysterious old trunk wedged in the corner.
Two auction workers maneuver it to the ladder,
remark on the weight, carefully hand it down.

Other sorters stop, wander over.
We gather, wipe away the grime,
joke about bodies, gold bars,
pry up the lid, lift out the top tray,

empty, lift out the next one, empty.

I ask, "What's the most unusual thing you've found?"
Two dusty men immediately lock eyes.
"Harold Bowen," says one. The other smiles.
"And we had to dig him out of the dumpster."

The old canvas bag with ashes
had not been recognized for what it was
until they stumbled upon the cremation papers
and had to search for Harold in the trash.

We laugh among things stored and forgotten.

The Auctioneer's Staff Sorts through WWII

I watch one worker kneel in the grass
taking a pocketknife to triage
father's WWII army uniform,
cutting away rotten bits,
saving most of the jacket.

He tells me what some things are,
ribbons from three campaigns,
a good conduct medal,
a sharp shooters medal,
which he carefully removes
to look at the back
to see if it is sterling.
It is. Forty bucks.
He pins it back on.

I tell nearby sorters the story
of how Dad met Patton.
After Normandy, D-Day,
he was an MP in occupied France,
guarding some road,
and told the lead driver
of one nighttime convoy:
no papers, no passing.
Dad outranked him. Then,
he told the sergeant the driver sent
that they were of equal status:
no papers, no passing,
and the officer the sarge sent forward
asked Dad's name when
Dad said the officer did not outrank his C.O.
Then a final figure strode up
through the shadows and said,
"God damn you, Sergeant Pete,
you son of a bitch, let us through!"

He did.

Proudest moment of my Dad's service,
being called a son of a bitch by General Patton.

They throw the scraps of uniform
into the semi-sized dumpster,
lay his jacket on the auction wagon,
move on to the next remnant.

Christmas in July

Sorting through the estate,
sweltering in summer heat,
I recognize the dented metal
Viking ship silhouette
mounted on wooden plaque,
a present from Uncle Curtis to my parents,
who proudly posed with it
for a Christmas Eve photograph,
then displayed the ship for years
in our suburban dining room,
and now passing through my hands,
worth barely a glance.

The Artist in the Barn Loft

The auction sorters
bring down from the loft
cases too heavy for me.
Outside in the sun,
they open cartons and bags to light
for the first time in years.

Brother-in-law Harlan's
old camera equipment,
thousands of dollars of
mechanical SLR cameras, lenses, filters,
one telephoto lens with a note,
"bought at garage sale, never used."
Polaroids, Canons, Minoltas,
large format negatives, developing
equipment, crowded slide reel.

The head auctioneer
uses his mobile phone
to take quick snaps of
once ultramodern instruments
that produced Harlan's
vanishing art.

Beginning with the Big Stuff

Estate sale movers
throw out five sofas
all of which at some point
I slept on—
Mount Prospect, Illinois,
Decorah, Iowa,
Eagle Mound, Wisconsin,
Eagle Point Trailer Court.

They dismantle
my sister and brother-in-law's
forty-five-year-old bedsprings
and sagging mattress.

Dreams vanish into
the yawning dumpster.

Halfway Through a Painful Chore—Sorting an Estate

I drink too much
Last night I drank
way too much
I slept late
am still hungover

I blame it on
the creative burst
re-born in me
the sudden need
to tell, to share

to remember
too many things
shared, then lost,
history known
to no one else.

Mice

We find dead mice everywhere
babies curled up in stuck drawers
adults under the porch couch
lying on their backs
tiny legs sticking straight up
like dead cartoon characters
mice corpses hiding
behind the basement toilet
in the shower stall
their shit trails
everywhere
over everything,
disgusting waste,
magnifying sorrow.

Additional Treasures

We take things from our own home
to add to the upcoming auction
of family possessions,

unused Christmas gifts
my unopened hummingbird mister,
husband Bill's beer making gift,

used golf clubs and putters,
collected Star Trek toys
(the phaser and tricorder),

toy trucks from my tomboy childhood,
a Tonka wrecker, pick-up whose front wheels turned
if you pressed the hood correctly.

toy semi for hauling grain,
a toy garage my father built for me,
a log cabin his father made for Dad,

a child-sized chair,
simple, hand-made rocking horse,
a Mouseketeer puppet,

the idle belongings
taking room in our house,
now taken to fill

the hollow spaces
amid the family
treasures.

Giving Things Away

In the living room
among boxes and bags and piles,
I've invited my women friends
to help themselves to grandmother's
quilts and doilies,
sister's never-used egg coddlers,
mom's silver appetizer forks,
Norwegian sweaters...

In the basement
my husband's friends
accept fishing lures,
barbecue tools, pliers,
extension cords, batteries...

I collect potential gifts
for other friends,
Jack Daniels playing cards,
fancy dishes, embroidered towels...

and useful empty notebooks,
unsent greeting cards, pens...

echoes, echoes, echoes...

Auction Morning

My childhood friend
of over fifty years
comes for the auction.

She keeps telling me,
"You should take this."
I say, "I have no room."

She points, "Don't you want this?"
"I don't need it," I say.
"I've taken my memory things."

The house is half empty now.
It's hard to watch the workers
discard things that won't sell—

a small wooden puffin,
a Norwegian bottle opener,
two tiny Asian puppet magnets,

a one-inch stuffed toy mole my husband
gave my sister, poster putty,
still usable.

I furtively fill my jacket pockets
with these last bits,
walk out on the lives

being sold.

Going. Going. Gone.

After the auction,
I wander through rooms
of unsold remainders.

Coat hangers in the closet
in the empty bedroom
where my father died.

Plastic pitchers on the counter
in the kitchen where
my brother-in-law died.

They were lucky to pass here.
Mother and sister died
in the same nursing home

ten miles away, fifteen years apart,
a few clothes left behind,
cat sweatshirt, stretch pants, fuzzy socks.

Unlike their men,
they did not die
where they loved

and were loved.

Empty

The house is hollow,
no laughter, no shouting,
silent, except for
my loud breathing.

I would fall
to my knees and weep,
but my arthritic knees
are too painful today.

I remember Christmases
and hot summers
and 4 p.m. happy hours
and Januarys making glög

I go downstairs and out
and begin to walk
one last time
up the wooded valley

past the bridge spanning
the dry creek bed
that becomes a torrent
when it flash floods

past the red barn
converted to summer cabin,
the green shed
that housed the pontoon

the fishing boat shed
home to duck decoys
and an old bicycle
from when I was age twelve.

I climb the rise where
flood waters have eaten away
half the grassy pass
where cars once drove

I walk to the end
of our property
and the farmer's fence
near where the old still was

and it is there, again,
I want to drop to my knees
and howl, howl again
merely, freely, howl,

frightening the birds
and small woodland creatures,
and then fall forward
hugging the earth

digging my fingers into the dirt
pressing my face into the
sweet smelling grass
tears streaming

like a flash flood
of my own making,
coming from a heart
that is breaking,

broken.
Instead I turn
and wend my way
slowly back to life.

Without Ceremony—Before the Sale

We scatter sister and her husband's ashes
over a clump of weeds and yellow wildflowers
that we believe are at the heart
of the plowed-under eagle mound
at the center of their valley home.

I pour Harlan out easy.
They forgot to seal him
in his protective plastic bag.
Sister Connie in her urn
is hermetically sealed.

My husband struggles
to open her, complaining
she's being difficult again,
just like always.

I try to be serious,
halfheartedly sing
a verse of Amazing Grace.

I thought I would be appalled
by the ashes on my fingertips.
I wipe them on the sweatpants
I donned this muggy summer day.

Harlan and Connie would laugh,
pleased we dressed for the occasion.

Do the Dead Care What We Do?

Shortly after she died,
I found sister's most recent journal
and put it away for later.
I could not bear to read it.

Two years later, after her husband died,
I found boxed journals going back decades
I glanced at first lines, usually
weather entries. "Today is cloudy..."

For weeks, the spiral notebooks
and hard-bound diaries sat silent
in my study, demanding attention.
I knew they were no *Walden*.
just a quiet life lived.

Today would I be trespasser?
Would she want me to read them?
We both public poets, yet shy persons?
I tore the pages out to recycle,
trashed wire binders and covers,

every tear, a tear.

No children, nieces, nephews, cousins…

I am tearing pages
out of my sister's journals
that cover over fifty years,
trying not to read them.

Inspired, I turn to my own files,
my grade school class pictures,
my report cards, old black and whites
of unidentified ancestors.

writings from my childhood
from high school
college
from yesterday.

I will be clean;
I will be whole;
I will be empty.

In the Old Steno Notebook

where I am writing these poems
Tyler's phone number appears
on the inside back cover.
He chauffeured my sister
from nursing home to clinic
where we met for appointments.

Here I noted
social services contacts,
nursing home rankings,
home services options
for her widowed husband,
funeral home numbers,
attorney numbers.

The pages are rumpled,
creased, ready to be tossed,
once I finish with these
poem scraps, four years of
monitoring illnesses,
dyings…

now it's just me,
tidying up the ends.

Resignation Affirmation

Winter nights I lie beneath
aunt's comforter and grandma's quilt,
the only soul left alive to know
the meaning of their weight and warmth.

Thrifty Norwegian

This summer I am using up my sister's
paper Christmas appetizer plates
and fall motif Thanksgiving napkins.
She would approve of things not going to waste.

I remember her price checking,
calculating nicest, but cheapest,
to satisfy her instinct to please
and save dollars that at the end

she never spent upon on herself.

Trailer Window Inheritance—Our New Summer Getaway

Looking west from
Wisconsin to Iowa,
impeccable beauty
few may see:
serene, tangerine,
chocolate-layered sunset
mirrored in
the Mississippi.

In this small piece
of saved inheritance,
I am blessed
remembering
my family,
gone now,
at peace

loving them.

Nancy Kay Peterson's poetry has appeared in print or online in numerous publications, most recently in *Lost Lake Folk Opera, One Sentence Poems, Spank the Carp, Steam Ticket, Tipton Poetry Journal* and *Three Line Poetry.* Two of her poems were nominated for The Pushcart Prize (2001 and 2002).

For five years, from 2004-2009, she co-edited and co-published the quarterly magazine *Main Channel Voices: A Dam Fine Literary Magazine* (Winona, MN). Her *Backwaters* column appeared at the end of each issue…just as the column *Headwaters* by co-publisher Carol Borzyskowski, began each issue.

Belated Remembrance, Peterson's first chapbook (Finishing Line Press, 2010), is a collection of poems telling the story of her great-great uncle Arne Kulterstad (1825-1902) who was convicted of murder in Norway and sentenced to be executed. He was saved by an editorial campaign by Bjørnstjerne Bjørnson, who later won the Nobel Prize in Literature. Arne was imprisoned in the Akerthus Fortress in Oslo. After some 20 years in prison, he was freed and exiled to Mount Horeb, Wisconsin. Her second chapbook, *Selling the Family* (Finishing Line Press, 2021), relates her experience in auctioning off her family's estate as the family's sole living descendent.

As a second-generation Norwegian-American, Peterson's childhood was rich in Norwegian traditions. Three out of four of her grandparents were born in Norway. One grandmother was born to Norwegian parents living in rural Minnesota, which was not unlike living in Norway. In their childhood homes, only Norwegian was spoken at home and at church. Hence, Peterson grew up with lutefisk, lefse, rosemaling and uff dahs.

Peterson was born in Madison, Wisconsin, and raised in the northwest Chicago suburbs. She earned an undergraduate degree in journalism from Southern Illinois University—Carbondale and a master's degree in Public Administration from Indiana State University in Terre Haute, Indiana. Most of her professional career involved writing and administering grants and public relations materials. In retirement, she began editing beginning author's novels. She credits her sister and fellow poet Connie Sanderson with encouraging her to take her own poetry more seriously and pursue publication. She lives in Winona, MN, with her husband, chemistry professor emeritus Dr. William C.B. Ng.

www.ingramcontent.com/pod-product-compliance
Lightning Source LLC
LaVergne TN
LVHW051022080826
845145LV00009B/2763

* 9 7 8 1 6 4 6 6 2 4 0 2 7 *